OZONE HOLE

Sally Morgan

SEA-TO-SEA

Mankato Collingwood London

This edition first published in 2010 by
Sea-to-Sea Publications
Distributed by Black Rabbit Books
P.O. Box 3263, Mankato, Minnesota 56002

Copyright © Sea-to-Sea Publications 2010

Printed in USA

Library of Congress Cataloging-in-Publication Data

Morgan, Sally.
  Ozone hole / Sally Morgan.
     p. cm. -- (Earth SOS)
  Includes index.
  ISBN 978-1-59771-224-8 (hardcover)
  1. Ozone layer depletion--Juvenile literature. 2. Ozone--Juvenile
literature. I. Title.
  QC879.712.M675 2010
  577.27'6--dc22

                              2008053159

9 8 7 6 5 4 3 2

Published by arrangement with the Watts
Publishing Group Ltd., London

EARTH SOS is based on the series EarthWatch published by Franklin Watts.
It was produced for Franklin Watts by Bender Richardson White,
P O Box 266, Uxbridge UB9 5NX.
Project Editor: Lionel Bender
Text Editor: Jenny Vaughan
Original text adapted and updated by: Jenny Vaughan
Designer: Ben White
Picture Researchers: Cathy Stastny and Daniela Marceddu
Media Conversion and Make-up: Mike Weintroub, MW Graphics,
and Clare Oliver
Production: Kim Richardson

Picture Credits Colorific!: page 29 left (Michael St. Maur Sheil).
Ecoscene: pages 4 (Nick Hawkes), 9 (Wayne Lawler), 21 bottom (Rob
Nicol). Environmental Images/Photo Library: pages 12 (Mike Midgley), 15
top (Jim Miles), 26 (Steve Morgan). Oxford Scientific Films: cover, small
photo (Konrad Wothe) and pages 1 (Ronald Toms), 6 top (Norbert
Rosing), 11 top (Kim Westerskov), 21 top (Warren Faidley). Panos
Pictures: pages 14 (Jim Holmes), 29 right. Planet Earth Pictures: pages 5
bottom, 13 bottom (Space Frontiers). Science Photo Library, London:
pages 5 top (NASA), 10 (David Parker), 13 top (NASA), 15 bottom
(Maximilian Stock Ltd), 17 (Simon Fraser), 20 (Simon Fraser), 25 top
(Simon Fraser). Stock Market Photo Library: cover main photo and pages
6 bottom (Zefa/Dick Durrance II), 8, 11 bottom (Frank Rossotto), 16, 18
(Benjamin Rondel), 19 left, 19 right (J. Bator), 22–23, 23, 25 bottom, 27
top, 27 bottom, 28. Telegraph Color Library: pages 22, 24.

Artwork by Raymond Turvey

Note to parents and teachers: Every effort has been made by the publisher to ensure that websites listed are suitable for children, that they are of the highest educational value, and that they contain no inappropriate or offensive material. However, because of the nature of the Internet, it is impossible to guarantee that the contents of these sites will not be altered. We strongly advise that Internet access is supervised by a responsible adult.

CONTENTS

THE OZONE HOLE

There is a layer of gas high above the Earth. This gas is ozone. It does an important job—it stops harmful rays from the Sun from reaching the Earth.

What is the ozone hole?

Ozone is very like the oxygen we breathe, but it has a strong smell. Chemicals used in factories can harm it. When this happens, the layer of ozone is so thin that scientists say there is an ozone hole. Harmful rays from the Sun can pass through the ozone hole.

Sunlight contains harmful rays, which can damage living things.

Putting it right

Scientists have been checking the ozone layer for many years. They know we can put things right if we stop using harmful chemicals.

Eco Thought

The size of the ozone hole changes. It was largest in 2002, over the Antarctic.

A picture of the Earth from space. The ozone layer is high above the clouds. The worst damage is over the Antarctic (at the bottom of the picture).

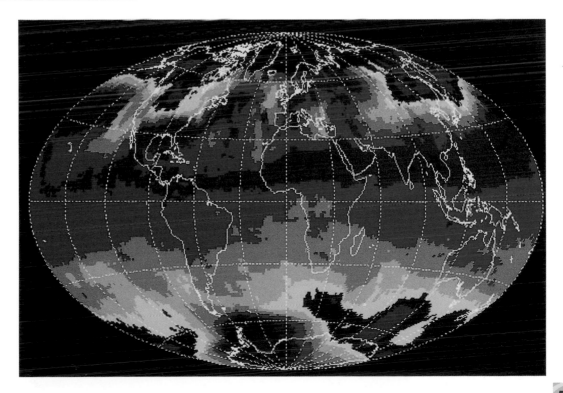

This is a computer picture of the Earth. The purple patches show where the ozone layer is thinnest.

THE ATMOSPHERE

The Earth is surrounded by a layer of air, called the atmosphere. The atmosphere reaches from the ground to 435 miles (700 km) above the Earth.

Layers of atmosphere

The bottom layer of the **atmosphere** is the **troposphere**. About three-quarters of all the gas in the atmosphere is in this layer. There is also **water vapor** in this layer. The next layer is the **stratosphere**. The ozone layer is here. The top layers are the **mesosphere** and the **thermosphere**.

As the Sun warms water, some turns into a gas called water vapor. Clouds form from this.

Balloons can fly very high, to where the air is colder and thinner.

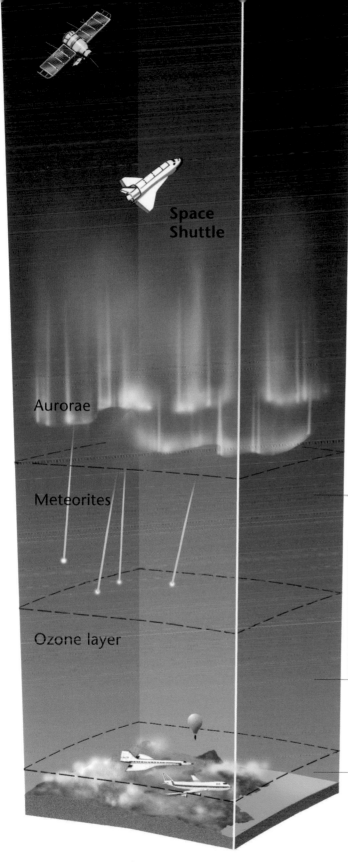

Space Shuttle

Aurorae

Meteorites

Ozone layer

THERMOSPHERE

MESOSPHERE

STRATOSPHERE

TROPOSPHERE

THE EARTH'S ATMOSPHERE
This picture shows the different layers in the Earth's atmosphere.

Air

The air we breathe is in the troposphere. It is mainly the gas nitrogen, but about one-fifth is oxygen. Most living things need this to stay alive. There are small amounts of other gases.

THE OZONE LAYER

The ozone is spread out unevenly in the ozone layer. It changes as light from the Sun breaks it up, and then it forms again.

Ultraviolet light

Sunshine brings us warmth and the light we use to see. It also contains invisible rays called **ultraviolet light**. This can damage living things. Ozone stops it from reaching us.

Rays of ultraviolet light from the Sun make our skin tan. Too much can burn us.

THE OZONE CYCLE
Everything is made of tiny **atoms**. Atoms link together and make **molecules**.

The molecules release heat when they split.

1. Ultraviolet rays break up the ozone molecules.

Oxygen atom

2. A molecule of oxygen and an atom of oxygen form.

3. The atom and the molecule join. They become ozone again.

Oxygen molecule

Good and bad ozone

Some factories and machines make ozone. It stays low in the atmosphere, and does not reach the ozone layer. It helps soak up the ultraviolet rays, but it can also make people's eyes and throats hurt. It is very bad for people with chest problems.

Try this
Sunglasses block out some ultraviolet rays from the Sun. Look around on a sunny day. Can you see better with sunglasses on? (Remember! Never look straight at the Sun.)

Sunglasses help protect our eyes from ultraviolet rays.

Eco Thought
The ozone layer is a few miles thick. If we could flatten it all together, it would be only ¼in (6mm) thick.

9

MEASURING OZONE

People have studied the weather for hundreds of years. They have been studying the atmosphere since the 1960s.

A scientist with a weather balloon.

Weather balloons

Scientists use weather balloons to find out what is happening in the lower atmosphere. The balloons float because they contain helium, which is lighter than air. The balloon carries a kind of radio called a **radio-sonde**. It sends information about the atmosphere back to Earth. This is put into computers, which measure the amounts of different gases in the atmosphere. Ozone was first measured in 1956.

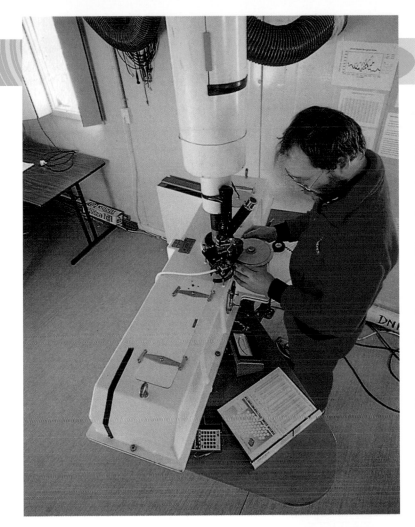

Using satellites

Scientists have been using weather satellites since the 1970s. These measure sea levels, air temperature, wind speeds, and the amount of water in the atmosphere. In 1978, the USA sent up the first satellite that could measure how thickly spread the molecules of ozone were.

A scientist measures how much ozone there is in a sample of air.

On the Ground

Scientists send up a weather balloon every day from the Antarctic. It measures ozone levels and can tell if ultraviolet rays are increasing.

Skylab was one of the first research stations in space. It sent information about the atmosphere back to Earth.

11

A DISCOVERY

In 1985, Dr. Joseph Farman discovered a hole in the ozone layer over the Antarctic.

Early warnings

In the 1970s, scientists found that certain chemicals damage ozone molecules. These are called ChloroFlouroCarbons (**CFCs**). These were once used in spray cans, but now they have been banned. In 1985, scientists found there was so little ozone over the Antarctic that they said there was an ozone hole. They found that this hole had first appeared in 1976.

This scientist is using a machine to measure ozone levels in the Antarctic.

Disappearing ozone

In the northern part of the world, there is not a big hole in the ozone. The ozone layer is getting thinner everywhere. It is thinnest over places where factories send out chemicals that harm ozone.

This computer image shows the South Pole. The red area is where there is so little ozone that we call it the ozone hole.

CFCS AND OZONE

Many chemicals that harm the ozone layer contain atoms of the gas chlorine. About three-quarters of all the chlorine in the air was put there by the actions of people. Most comes from CFCs.

Wonder chemicals

CFCs were invented in the 1920s. People called them "wonder chemicals." They are cheap to make and last a long time. Also, they are not poisonous. At first, they were used in spray cans, in refrigerators, and for making the bubbles in **polystyrene** foam. CFCs were so useful that huge amounts were made. Most were made in the USA. People went on using CFCs for 50 years. Then scientists realized that they were having a bad effect on the ozone layer.

Polystyrene boxes help keep things cold. They are light and strong, but making them can release CFCs.

Drifting upward

CFCs travel up through the air. They reach the stratosphere and the ozone layer. This can take ten years. After that, they break down. They release chlorine atoms, which can attack ozone molecules.

Spray cans like this used to have CFCs in them. This damaged the ozone layer, so modern cans use different gases.

Eco Thought
Scientists think that in 1988, more than 1 million tons (1 billion kg) of CFCs reached the upper atmosphere.

*A worker in an **electronics** factory. Factories like this release a lot of CFCs into the air.*

ABOUT OZONE

In the ozone layer, ozone is made and destroyed all the time. This means there should always be the same amount of ozone. Ozone holes form if chemicals like CFCs destroy too much ozone too fast.

What happens in the ozone layer?

Oxygen molecules are made up of two oxygen atoms. Ozone molecules are made up of three. Ultraviolet light splits up some oxygen molecules. Ozone forms when the spare atoms join with oxygen. Ultraviolet light also breaks up ozone molecules, to help form oxygen (see page 8). So the amount of ozone says the same, unless CFCs are released.

Suntan lotion can protect us from harmful ultraviolet rays.

Eco Thought
Some CFCs can last for 200 years, and one CFC molecule can destroy 100,000 molecules of ozone.

What do CFCs do?

When CFCs reach the stratosphere, ultraviolet light breaks them down. They set free atoms of chlorine. These help change ozone into oxygen molecules and oxygen atoms. We say chlorine is a **catalyst**. A catalyst makes something happen, but does not change itself.

HOW CFCs DAMAGE THE OZONE LAYER

Fluorocarbon

Ultraviolet light from the sun

Heat is released as ozone molecule splits

CFC molecule splits apart

Free chlorine atom

Ozone molecule

Oxygen molecule

Chlorine atom can attack more ozone

breaks down

Oxygen atom

Oxygen atom—joins with chlorine atom

A scientist is measuring the level of CFCs in the atmosphere.

OTHER DANGERS

CFCs are not the only chemicals that harm the ozone layer. There are many others, too.

Aircraft engines

Jet aircraft produce chemicals called nitrogen oxides. These make ozone break down faster. They do not get used up as this happens, so they can go on and damage more ozone.

Eco Thought
Passenger jets release about 3.5 million tons (3.5 billion kg) of nitrogen oxides every year.

The Space Shuttle

Rockets launch the Space Shuttle. These give off the gas hydrogen chloride. It is given off when **volcanoes** erupt, too. It contains chlorine, which breaks down ozone molecules.

When Concordes flew, they used to release ozone-harming gases straight into the stratosphere.

Hydrogen chloride gas reaches the ozone layer when the Space Shuttle is launched.

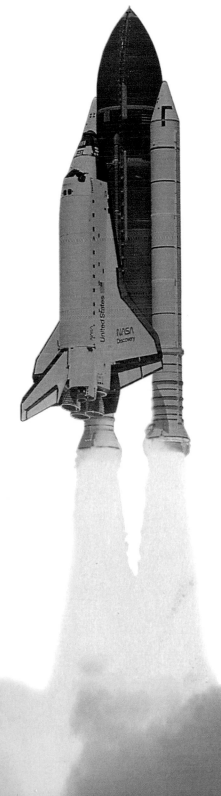

When an aircraft sprays crops, harmful chemicals stay in the air.

Pesticides and dry cleaning

Farmers spray chemicals on their crops to kill insects and **fungi.** We call these **pesticides**. Many contain a chemical called methyl bromide. This contains a gas that is like chlorine, which can attack ozone. When we have clothes dry cleaned, chemicals containing chlorine are used. This can cause damage to the ozone layer, too.

19

NATURAL CAUSES

Not all chlorine is produced by people. Some comes naturally from forest fires and from volcanoes, when they erupt.

Erupting volcanoes

When a volcano erupts, it sends water vapor and chemicals high into the air. One of the chemicals is hydrogen chloride, which is made up of hydrogen and chlorine. Chlorine damages ozone.

Erupting volcanoes send chemicals into the atmosphere.

Volcanic clouds

Scientists have studied the clouds of chemicals that some volcanoes sent into the air. They used weather balloons, aircraft, and satellites. They found that ice in the troposphere got rid of most of the hydrogen chloride in the clouds. A small amount reached the ozone layer, and damaged it.

Eco Thought

Mount Pinatubo erupted in 1991. This may have made the ozone hole over the Antarctic grow by one-fifth.

Lightning and fires

Lightning is a huge spark of electricity in the sky. When lightning happens high in the atmosphere, it can split ozone molecules, and make the ozone layer thinner. On the ground, big forest fires release many different gases. Some of these can harm the ozone layer.

Lightning makes ozone from oxygen, and also makes chemicals that attack ozone.

Forest fires release gases into the air. These can harm the ozone layer.

INSIDE THE HOLE

The ozone hole appears in the Antarctic every year at the end of winter. The hole then grows larger all through the spring.

Cut off from the world

Antarctic winters are very cold. Strong winds cut off the air from the rest of the world. The water in the air turns into ice. This helps chlorine attack ozone molecules. When spring comes, the Sun's rays sends out ultraviolet light. They break up CFCs and make more chlorine. Ozone is destroyed.

Clouds are made up of tiny droplets of water. When these get very cold, they become ice crystals.

When water freezes in the air, it forms ice crystals. These make ozone break up faster.

The hole breaks up

In November, winds carry warm air to the Antarctic. These have ozone in them, so the hole disappears. But some air with very little ozone in it drifts north to countries such as Australia.

A scientist checks the ultraviolet light reaching these crops.

An Arctic hole?

The weather in the Arctic is different from the Antarctic. Instead of a hole, the ozone layer there can get very thin.

THE EFFECTS ON US

Ultraviolet light helps our bodies make vitamin D. We need this chemical for healthy bones. But too much ultraviolet light harms us in many ways.

Sensitive eyes

Ultraviolet light can harm our eyes, so that we can no longer see properly. Sunglasses protect our eyes. This is why we should always wear them in bright light.

This girl is having her eyes checked. Ultraviolet light can harm our eyes.

Eco Thought

Scientists in the USA think that if we go on destroying ozone, 50,000 more people every year will get skin **cancer**. Around 100,000 more will go blind because of ultraviolet rays.

Cancer cells

We absorb ultraviolet rays through our skin. When this happens, our skin burns. If this happens too often, cancer cells form in our skin. Skin cancer is getting more common in southern countries, such as Australia. It affects animals, too.

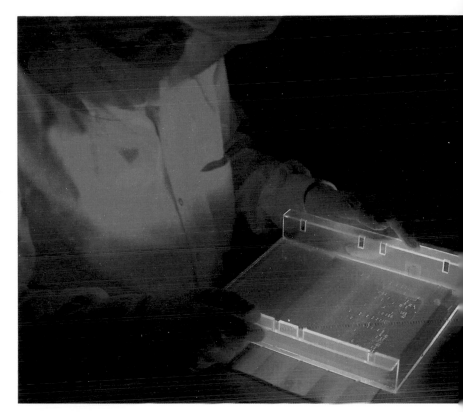

A scientist uses ultraviolet light to study DNA. DNA is a chemical in body cells. Ultraviolet rays harm it.

A scientist studies human cells that have been harmed by ultraviolet light.

On the Ground

In Australia they say:
SLIP on some clothes
SLAP on a hat
SLOP on suntan lotion. Doing this will protect you from the Sun's dangerous rays.

FIXING THE HOLE

We have to stop using CFCs and other chemicals that harm the ozone layer.

If the ozone layer starts to grow thicker again, we will notice it first in the Antarctic.

International agreements

In 1987, 31 countries signed an agreement called the Montreal Protocol. They agreed to cut back on CFCs so that, soon, no one will use them any more. They also agreed to cut back on other harmful gases.

On the Ground

People who have **asthma** used to use inhalers with CFCs in them. In 1998, scientists found a better chemical to use instead.

Other chemicals

HFCs are a kind of chemical that people can use instead of CFCs. But there is a problem with HCFs. They may be helping to change the climate. There are also substances called **hydrocarbons** that can be used instead of CFCs. Hydrocarbons contain a substance called carbon. They do no harm, and they work as well as CFCs.

These new refrigerators work without using CFCs.

This man is making air conditioning machines that do not use CFCs.

Eco Thought

The CFCs that were released in the 1980s and 1990s have just reached the ozone layer. Soon, the levels there may be higher than ever before. But they may be back to normal by 2045.

WHAT CAN WE DO?

Scientists think the ozone layer will be mended by 2050. But this will only happen if people all over the world stop using harmful chemicals.

Farming and factories

Chemicals that damage ozone are still used in factories and by farmers. It is important to cut back on how much of these chemicals are used. We can make choices that will help, too.

This is a dump in the USA. Poisonous wastes, such as CFCs, can be left safely here.

Refrigerators

When we get rid of old refrigerators, we can make sure any harmful chemicals are taken away safely. We can also make sure that the new refrigerator we are buying does not contain any CFCs.

This street seller is selling secondhand parts from electronic machines. This means fewer new machines need to be made.

The cooling substance in old refrigerators contains CFCs. This man is getting rid of it safely.

On the Ground

In Ghana, people buy a lot of old refrigerators. These contain CFCs. Local people change them, so they use fewer harmful chemicals.

FACT FILE

By 2030

More than 100 countries signed a new agreement in 1992. They included more than nine-tenths of all the people in the world who were using CFCs. They agreed to get rid of all CFCs and other chemicals like them by the year 2030.

Worse than we expected

Ozone is being destroyed over parts of the world where many people live. In 1991, American scientists found out that this was three times worse than they thought. It was especially bad over North America and Europe.

Ultraviolet light

There are three kinds of ultraviolet rays: UVA, UVB, and UVC. UVA does the least damage, UVC does the most. Ozone manages to stop all UVC. UVB is weakest when sunlight has to travel through the most atmosphere. This happens at the North and South Poles. Most UV-B is found around the equator. People there get 1,000 times more.

Measuring ozone

We measure ozone in Dobson units. One Dobson unit is about 27 million molecules of ozone per 0.15 square inch (1 square cm).

Websites

http://www.epa.gov/
http://kids.national geographic.com
http://www.atm.ch. cam.ac.uk/tour/

GLOSSARY

Asthma A problem some people have with their lungs that makes it hard to breathe.

Atmosphere The layer of gases around the Earth.

Atom The tiniest part of a substance.

Cancer A disease where some of the cells that make up our bodies grow out of control.

Catalyst A substance that speeds up the way chemicals affect each other. It does not change itself.

CFCs Short for ChloroFluorocarbons: gases that were once used in spray cans and refrigerators (fridges).

Electronics Machines, such as computers, and calculators that have circuit boards in them.

Fungi Tiny living things that make mushrooms and toadstools.

Hydrocarbons Chemicals that contain the gas hydrogen and the substance carbon. Natural gas, coal, and oil are all hydrocarbons.

Mesosphere The third highest layer of the atmosphere.

Molecule Two or more atoms linked together.

Pesticide A substance used on crops to kill pests.

Poles (North and South) The North Pole is the very farthest point north on Earth. The South Pole is the very farthest point south.

Polystyrene A light material that does not bend. It is used for packing and for insulating things—keeping them warm or cold.

Radio-sonde A balloon used by scientists to study weather conditions high in the atmosphere.

Satellite An object that is sent into space, and that orbits the Earth or another planet.

Space Shuttle A spacecraft that is sent into space using rockets, but can land afterward like an aircraft.

Stratosphere The second-highest layer of the atmosphere.

Thermosphere The highest layer of the atmosphere.

Troposphere The bottom layer of the atmosphere.

Ultraviolet light Invisible rays that come from the Sun, and which can harm us.

Volcano A hole in the outer crust of the Earth. Hot rocks and gas may escape through it into the atmosphere.

Water vapor Water in the form of a gas.

INDEX